The Gittings Photographs

Arthur Gittings c. 1909

During 1995, a hoard of some 700 half-plate photographic negatives was found in the roof space of the old cottage and corner shop, next to the Tickled Trout public house in Wye, when the son of the new owner was exploring the attic. Amazingly, the glass plates had remained untouched for at least fifty years despite many changes of tenant and owner, even when the building was being re-roofed. Recognizing that they would be of considerable local interest, the owner, Graham Miller, presented them to the Wye Historical Society.

All the plates were extremely dirty and the task of sorting and cleaning them was begun by the late Henry Haste. Although a number were broken, stuck together, or showed damage to the emulsion, most of the negatives were in remarkably good condition and many were perfect. Henry discovered that they were the work of Arthur Gittings who had traded from the corner shop and established himself as the village photographer during the early years of this century.

Since Henry's death, many more of the negatives have been investigated and local people have been interviewed to try to discover as much as possible about Arthur Gittings and his photographs.

Articles written by members of Wye Historical Society in *Wye Local History* and the Wye Parish Magazines for the years 1900 to 1925, have also been invaluable sources of information about the events and people shown in the photographs.

Advertisement from Wye Parish Magazine , 1918

Arthur Gittings - a Village Photographer

Edwin Arthur Gittings was born in 1882 at 'Longley House', 2 Church Street, Wye. He was the second youngest of seven children (five boys and two girls). His father, Colin Gittings, was a coal merchant who operated from a depot at the railway station in Bramble Lane and kept his horses in a field between Honeysuckle Cottage and Bramble Farmhouse. The late Mrs Peggy Amos built a house on this site which she called 'Gittings'.

The old house opposite the station, now 'Honeysuckle Cottage' with the Kemsley family. Arthur Gittings believed he had been born here; his father kept his horses in the field which adjoined the garden on the right.

Colin Gittings came from a well-established Gillingham family. His father, Captain Henry Gittings RN, had fourteen children. He sent two of his sons, Colin and Henry jr, to sea as midshipmen and in 1845, Henry was a member of the crew of the ketch *Vision* on a plant-collecting voyage off Australia. He and three others went ashore on an island and were murdered by the natives. Worried that the same thing might happen to Colin, his family bought him out of the Navy. Colin joined the London, Chatham and Dover Railway as a clerk and was present at the opening of Waterloo Station (he did a painting of the event). In 1872 he married Charlotte Maria Cloke, at Waltham. Charlotte's father, Thomas Cloke, was the village grocer and postmaster and owned a freehold house and the mill behind on Kake Street. The couple lived in the West Gate area of Canterbury where two sons, also named Henry and Colin, were born. But, by 1875 Colin Gittings was listed in Kelly's Directory as a coal merchant employing three men at the depot at Wye Station; and the family was living in Longley House.

During the next ten years, two daughters, Charlotte and Emma were born, followed by three sons, Walter, Edwin Arthur and Charles. When Colin Gittings died aged fifty-three in 1896 Arthur Gittings was only fourteen. To support the family his mother became a dressmaker and was still advertising in Kelly's Directory in 1903. After her death in 1906 Arthur's sister, also called Charlotte, carried on the business until about 1938. Charlotte and Emma Gittings continued to live at Longley House into old age and were well known in the village where they were referred to as 'Trett' and 'Trott'.

By 1902, Arthur was working as town postman and living with his mother and sisters in Longley House, which they rented from Miss Hudson whose family had a farm at Hastingleigh. (Her brother was Minister of Agriculture during WWII.)

Arthur Gittings in his uniform as Town Postman c. 1909. His older brother, Walter, became a postman in Ashford.

Arthur Gittings had very poor eyesight, and when medicals for postmen were introduced, he had to leave the postal service and was virtually unemployable.

Despite this disability, he developed an interest in photography, became the village photographer and was present at all the local events. The money he earned enabled him to start his own business and he moved to the cottage next to the 'Victoria Inn' (now the Tickled Trout), set up a darkroom in a cupboard, and opened his shop.

The window of the corner shop, 7 Bridge Street, showing Gittings's photographs. Later this became a general store although Gittings continued to develop films for other people. The station building can be seen in the background.

In October 1916 Arthur Gittings married Kate Edith Bennett, whose brother Frederick, was butler at Olantigh House on the northern outskirts of Wye. He advertised his business in Wye Parish Magazine in March 1917 and in Kelly's Directory in 1918. This was probably his most productive period; for, as more people acquired their own cameras, he provided a developing service and did less of his own photography.

By 1922 Arthur Gittings is listed in Kelly's as 'shopkeeper', 5 Bridge Street and 'photographer', 7 Bridge Street. He traded from the corner shop, selling groceries, confectionery, tobacco and other commodities. His approach must have been very professional: a villager, who was a young lad at that time said, 'even if his sight was bad he never gave an extra sweet as an overweight'. He was able to cut small pieces of slab toffee so that the weight was correct. Gittings was given the nickname 'Ding' by village children because of the sound of his shop bell.

He and his wife had one daughter, Phyllis, and the family lived in the cottage next to the shop until about 1935 when Gittings sold the shop to Helen Bailey and they moved to 45 Scotton Street. Twenty years later they moved to Ashford to be near relatives. Arthur died, aged seventy-five, in 1958.

Arthur's older brother, Walter Gittings, with his wife and son, Herbert Leslie, outside 27 Providence Street, Ashford, c. 1913. Walter Gittings worked as a postman in Ashford.

Arthur Gittings used a half-plate camera made of mahogany with brass fittings and a black fabric bellows, which he bought from Alfred Lepper.

Almost all of his photographs were taken outside using natural light, and they are often posed against makeshift backgrounds; a curtain or board was propped against a wall, or the wall alone was used. He made use of various props: the same piece of carpet, backcloth, table or chair, sometimes painted scenery and even his own tripod, are seen in a number of his photographs (see photo of Gittings as a postman on the previous page). In many instances, the background of a photograph provides a glimpse of the village environment at that time, or has given a clue as to when the photograph was taken.

After the death of Arthur's grandfather in Waltham, his uncle took over the village shop and mill on Kake Street. Arthur would cycle out to visit his mother's family with his camera strapped to his bicycle. Many of the photographs he took of the surrounding areas are well known to collectors of local postcards. Unfortunately, not all of the negatives for these have survived.

Among the photographs are some charming studies of animals, like this one of the family cat, seemingly oblivious to the young bird. (*The damage to the emulsion at bottom left is also seen in other photographs*).

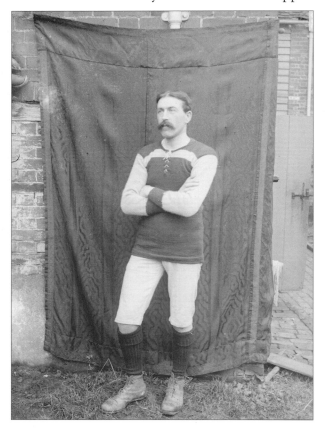 

These photographs of Arthur Gittings in football strip and of a woman and baby (probably his sister-in-law, Mrs Walter Gittings with Herbert) were taken in 1908, at the back of 2 Church Street. The courtyard behind this house and 2 Bridge Street has seen several changes. At that time, there was a single-storey building opposite the Vicarage and the doctor's house, 'Fieldview', (now the Library and the Wife of Bath restaurant). The guttering on the roof of this building, which was used as the doctor's surgery, can just be seen top left in Arthur's photograph. The collection contains a number of other photographs taken here.

Waltham

Left: The 'Lord Nelson' public house at Waltham has recently been sold as a private residence. Gittings would cycle from his grandfather's shop on Kake Street, down Church Lane, past the pub and the church where his parents were married, and into the valley known as 'Duckpit'. From there he would cycle through Evington and Brabourne and back to Wye along the 'Pilgrims' Way' at the foot of the Downs; or he would return through Crundale and past Olantigh, where his brother-in-law worked.

Right: 'Little Buckets Farm', Waltham. This scene of flooding along Duckpit Road probably took place in the autumn of 1909 when there was unusually heavy rainfall and 5.99ins fell in three days over East Kent.
Little Buckets Farm is still recognisable today.

Left: This scene of flooding along 'Duckpit' below Yockletts Bank, is also believed to have been during the autumn of 1909. A 'nailbourne' runs along the valley bottom which floods when the watertable rises - hence its name of 'Duckpit'. Flooding is now uncommon; possibly due to the increased demand for water from the underlying chalk.

Brabourne

Above: The entrance to Saint Mary's churchyard, Brabourne, with 18th century cottages. The photograph is taken from the field which was then opposite. The village shop, now a private house, can be seen on the left.

Right: The Forge, Brabourne, stands on Canterbury Road along from the 'Five Bells' public house. It is recognisable today by the plaque above the door.

Below: Egerton Cottages, opposite the Five Bells, belonged to the Finn family, who were carpenters, wheelwrights and undertakers.

Arthur Gittings also spent a considerable amount of time at Olantigh, courting his future wife who worked there with her brother, and Arthur was able to take an extensive series of photographs of the house and its grounds. Many of his photographs were published by Henry Mummery, who owned Wye Post Office on the corner of the Green and Church Street, Wye.

Olantigh

The Olantigh estate lies along Olantigh Road to the north of Wye. The name is ancient and means 'Holly Enclosure'. Cardinal Kempe, the founder of Wye College, was born in a house on the site in 1380, but, at the beginning of this century, a large Georgian mansion (built in 1767) stood there. This was the home of Wye's 'Squire', Wanley Ellis Sawbridge Erle-Drax and his family. In the nineteenth century, the house had been owned by his uncle, John Samuel Wanley Sawbridge-Erle-Drax. He had changed the name of the house to 'Olantigh Towers' and, among other alterations, had added three picture galleries to house his collection.

In December 1903 a disastrous fire destroyed most of the Georgian mansion and WES Erle-Drax commissioned the Architects, Messrs Brown and Burnett, of Birmingham, to rebuild the house on a smaller scale. The work was completed in 1912. Although the picture galleries were protected by fire curtains and survived the fire, only one was retained in the new house.

This equestrian statue of John Samuel Wanley Sawbridge-Erle-Drax was originally in front of the house. It now stands to the east, near the gates. He was a colourful character, nicknamed 'The Mad Major', who was said to have been able to jump his horse over both gates of the level crossing at Wye station.

Left: Detail of the fountain which replaced the Hubert fountain. Only the top portion is now visible in the centre of the pond in front of the house.

New Olantigh from the north, showing the portico which survived the fire of 1903. The fountain replaced a much larger one, the Hubert Fountain (now in Victoria Park, Ashford), which was bought from the Olantigh Estate and presented to the town in 1911 by George Harper, an Ashford businessman.

While the house was being rebuilt, the Erle-Drax family moved to Withersdane Hall, then to 'Glenthorne' (now 'James Wyllie House'), Upper Bridge Street in Wye; and later to Bilting House. They did not return to Olantigh and, in 1913, WES Erle-Drax leased the House to James Hope Loudon who moved in with his wife Louise Wilhelmina and their two young children, Connie and Billy (the late Francis William Hope Loudon). In 1935, James Hope Loudon bought the Olantigh estate: on his death it passed to his son Billy and is still owned by his grandson.

During their ownership, the Loudons have made changes to the house, including the removal of the remaining picture gallery.

Olantigh House from the east, c. 1914. The building on the left housed the picture gallery which was demolished and replaced by the present terrace and swimming pool in 1960. On the right can be seen the lower end of the formal garden.

Mrs Loudon (*second left*) with Connie (*left*) and Billy Loudon on the balcony outside the picture gallery, c. 1914. The identities of the other two women are not known. The statue was bought in 1851 at the Great Exhibition in Hyde Park.

Above: The interior of the Picture Gallery, c.1914.
Left; This picture, numbered 62, hangs in the centre of the wall far right.

Arthur's brother-in-law, Frederick Bennett, was butler at Olantigh at the beginning of WWI, and was said to have been 'interested in anything new' and to have encouraged Arthur's interest in photography. After WWI, Frederick and his family moved to North Kent for him to work in the Aircraft industry.

Right: Frederick Bennett, Arthur's brother-in-law and butler at Olantigh, with his family outside Little Olantigh farmhouse, c. 1916. *Left to right;* Frederick and Leonard, his wife Louie with Margaret Ena. (They had a further son, Douglas).

9

Right: The formal garden to the east of the house, c. 1914. This photograph was one of a series published as postcards when the house was still referred to as 'Olantigh Towers'. *Above:* one of the decorative urns in the garden.

Left: Olantigh gardens - bridge over the River Stour. Olantigh House is on the far left. The bridge has been replaced several times, but the 18th Century statues of a shepherd and shepherdess remain. (The shepherd is the subject of the drawing by John Ward, which is used as the logo for Stour Music).

Left: The weir at Olantigh. In the past, an ancient mill stood near here - thought to have been a fulling mill. The sluice, seen on the left, may have been at the end of the mill race .

John Bond, head gardener at Olantigh, in the greenhouse at Little Olantigh. He was an outstanding plantsman and won many prizes for JH Loudon at local and national events. In the twenties, he helped Mrs Loudon redesign the gardens.

Mrs Loudon and Connie Loudon seated below the balcony at Olantigh. In January 1918 Connie married Captain HC LLoyd, MC who was Adjutant at the aerodrome on Bramble Lane. Wye Parish Magazine recorded the event and reported, 'a guard of honour appeared in the air, and pilots from their aeroplanes waved their good wishes'.

Arthur Gittings particularly enjoyed visiting 'Little Olantigh' on the slopes above Olantigh, to get damsons, which he said, 'set me up for the winter'. He had many friends among the people who worked on the Olantigh estate. They included John Bond, the head gardener, who lived at Little Olantigh, and the family of William Hann who was tenant of the farm at Little Olantigh.

Above: Lionel Edwards, groom at Olantigh, in front of the ivy-covered walls of the farmhouse.
Left: Ray Hubbard, son of WES Erle-Drax's gamekeeper.

Left: Irene and George Hann, the youngest of William and Elizabeth Hann's large family, with their dog, Rex, at the farmhouse, Little Olantigh, c. 1916.

Right: Arthur Gittings's photographs of children are particularly appealing – like this study of children with a basket of flowers. Small children found it difficult to keep still for the time needed for the exposures and so their expressions are often very serious. It was unusual for a child to be photographed without shoes!

The Parish Church of St Gregory and St Martin, Wye

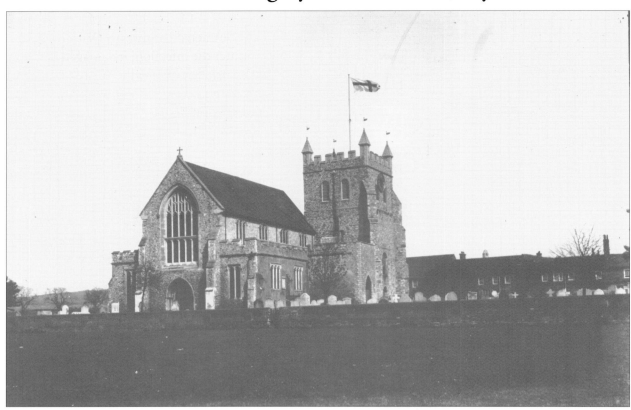

Above: This photograph of Wye Church was used on the cover of the Parish Magazine from 1916 to 1923 when it was followed by another view, also by Gittings. It shows the church before the the graveyard was extended on to the Churchfield at the end of WW I ; and before the development of the Churchfield Way estate after WWII. The Victorian west window (seen here) was damaged by a land mine which fell on the Churchfield during WW II and was replaced with the present window. The College buildings can be clearly seen in the background as there were fewer and smaller trees in the churchyard (the cherry trees along the path to the south door were planted after WWII in memory of those who did not return).

Left: Canon Lambert and family in the garden of the Vicarage, c. 1915. The Rev Canon Edgar Lambert was vicar of Wye from December 1911 to December 1926. He had been in the Navy, was a great sportsman and encouraged young people to take part in cricket and football.
Left to right, back row: Rachel Lambert, Canon Lambert, Mrs Lambert, Captain JEH Lambert, and Hilda Lambert.
Front row: The younger brothers: Roger, Stephen and Denis.

Right: Rear of the Vicarage, (now the Library), Upper Bridge Street. The grounds have now been developed to provide sheltered housing in 'Little Kempes' and parking for the library staff. Some of the beautiful chestnut trees remain. Many social and fund-raising events took place here in Canon Lambert's time and when the previous vicar, the Rev. Seymour Henry Rendall, was incumbent. The Rev. SH Rendall's mother lived at the Vicarage until her death in July 1905; he married in July 1908, and left Wye in 1911.

Left: This photograph is said to have been taken at a fete on Empire Day 1905. However, the Parish Magazine for that year, only mentions a Temperance Fete planned for Whit Monday, which had to be postponed until August bank holiday because of the serious illness of the Rev. S H Rendall's mother. The first event , then, was a Maypole dance. (A maypole can just be seen to the left of the house in front of the trees.)

Right: Nurse Martin with Mr and Mrs Henry Mummery and their new son, George, in 1905. Did Nurse Martin deliver him? Behind her is Charles Taylor who had a cycle shop on the Green. He lodged with the Mummerys who owned the Post Office on the corner of the Green and Church Street.

One of the causes supported by village fund-raising activities was the Wye District Nursing Association which, from public subscriptions and money raised at fetes, jumble sales and concerts, paid for a district nurse. Nurse Martin was appointed in 1903 and continued as district nurse and midwife until forced to retire by ill health in 1916. The salary for a 'long-trained' nurse was £60-£70 a year at the time of her appointment.

Fetes and pageants were usually held in the gardens of large houses in the village; such as the Vicarage, Oxenturn House or Withersdane Hall. Choir outings and Sunday-school treats went further afield: to Olantigh, Eastwell Park, farms on the Downs, or even to Margate, Hastings and Folkestone.

Above: Hester Dunstan (daughter of the Principal of the SEAC) in costume for one of the fund-raising pageants.

Above: Winner of one of the babyshows at a Temperance Fete held in the Vicarage garden ?

Above: Wedding photograph of an unknown couple. Ben Burnham is 2nd, and Alfred Lepper 5th from the left in the back row. The only concession to the occasion - a mat under the couples' feet; and the family pet is present.

Left: The interior of All Saints Church, Boughton Aluph, c. 1914.

Familiar to participants of the Stour Music Festival, the church is currently undergoing a programme of repair and restoration, paid for by grants from various bodies and local fund raising. It received a grant from English Heritage in 1988; and has just been awarded a Heritage Lottery Grant towards re-roofing. The church was badly damaged by incendiary bombs dropped by a lone German bomber on 16 September 1940, the day after the Battle of Britain, but was saved by the action of Wye Fire Brigade. A plaque in the church commemorates this. The pews were removed c. 1956.

Right: Cottages at Boughton Lees opposite the green and the cricket pitch. Matches were played here against Wye Cricket Club. (The building in front has been converted into four separate dwellings).

Above: Eastwell Park, c. 1914, now known as Eastwell Manor. Before WWI it was owned by M King, a diamond merchant, who made its grounds available for Sunday school outings and such occasions. Children from Wye were taken there by cart.

The building seen here, with its conservatory on the right, dated from 1893 when Eastwell House was enlarged by William, 2nd Lord Gerard. In turn this Victorian Mansion was demolished by Sir John de Fonblanque Pennefather, Bart., and rebuilt 1926-8 to a design by BC Deacon. The manor of Eastwell goes back to Saxon times. It was the seat of the Earls of Winchilsea and remained in the family of Finch Hatton for 257 years. During the latter part of the nineteenth century it was rented by Prince Alfred Duke of Edinburgh, the second son of Queen Victoria; his daughter, Princess Marie Alexandra Victoria who became Queen of Romania, was born here in 1875.

Wye Racecourse

George Kennett originally held races at Fanscombe and opened Wye racecourse in 1881 on land behind Harville Farmhouse, the entrance being from Harville Road alongside the pond. It was one of the shortest courses in England - a mile round, with brush fences, a water jump and an inner parallel course for hurdle racing. There were all the amenities including a grandstand, stabling for visiting horses and a weighing room.

Except for breaks during the two world wars, races were held on Mondays in September, January, March and May, until 1975.

The proximity of Wye station helped to increase the popularity of the races, and regular 'racing specials' were run from London (In 1911, fares were 11/- First Class and 7/- Second Class). Village children were given permission to leave school early on race days before the crowds came out from the races, and were usually able to get in through a gap in the hedge to watch the last race.

George Kennet died in 1904 and racing was carried on by his three sons. By 1924 two had died and Richard, the survivor, took as partner John Long who purchased the course in 1934.

Racing finished in 1975 when, after increasing reports of accidents, conditions on the course were considered too dangerous. Officials from the Jockey Club inspected the course and refused to renew the licence until alterations to improve safety were carried out. The owners were unable to afford to have the work done and the racecourse was forced to close.

Above: Harville Farmhouse with Frank Kennett and his wife. c. 1915. (Frank was one of George Kennett's sons).

Right: Stable lads at Harville racecourse c. 1912. The grandstand can be seen in the background.

In the early days of Wye Cricket Club, matches were played on the racecourse; and during WWI the stables were used to house the horses of troops stationed in Wye.

The South Eastern Railway and Wye Station

A line from Ashford to Canterbury West and the Thanet towns was approved by Parliament in 1844 at an estimated cost of nearly £390, 000. It was designed by Joseph Cubitt and constructed by Messrs Miller and Blackie (Liverpool). The line was opened on Friday, 6 February 1846, when a special train with eighteen carriages, headed by locomotives 'Mars' and 'Orion', left London at ten o'clock to drive through Kent.

At first, the line was part of the South Eastern Railway; then, from January 1899 until 1923, part of the South Eastern and Chatham Railway. In 1923, four large railway companies were formed and the SECR became one of the major parts of the Southern Railway. (It is now part of Connex South Eastern.)

To avoid the expense of constructing bridges and tunnels, level crossings were used; and Parliament approved a fine, of £5, for the directors of the company if road traffic was kept waiting for more than 5 minutes at the level crossing at Wye. Moreover, trains were expected to halt at the crossing until the road traffic had cleared.

Because the platform was too short, third class passengers had to dismount on to a box. Students returning to the College from the station were told 'to progress quietly not to disturb the residents in Bridge Street'. (Little has changed).

The railway made travel easy and outings were arranged to take advantage of special excursion fares to seaside towns like Margate, Folkestone and Hastings: even to events in London. On racedays, there was a stall by the gatehouse cottage which sold jellied eels and whelks to the racegoers.

Staff at Wye station, outside the shelter on the down platform, February 1913. The photograph was taken when Geer, the Station Master who lived at the station, was promoted and left the village.
Back row: Tom Lusted (signalman); Unknown; Bill Vidler (signalman); ? Hann; Geer (Stationmaster).
Front: Godden (gateman) lived in the gatehouse; Bill Hann; Unknown (signalman) had an allotment by the station; George Darrell (gateman) lived 63 Bridge Street. Note the posters.

Wye College

Wye College and Grammar School were founded by Cardinal Kempe in 1447. The Grammar school survived the Dissolution of the Monasteries in 1545 and the southern part of the medieval College buildings, the garden and the old 'Latin School' building on the High Street were reserved for its Master and boys. The Old Hall, the Parlour and the Wheelroom were occupied by the schools founded and endowed by Lady Joanna Thornhill and Sir George Wheler during the 18th century. The Grammar School was forced to close through bankruptcy in 1889, and was replaced by a private school operating from the Latin School. In 1893, the County Councils of Kent and Surrey acquired the College buildings for a South-Eastern Agricultural College (SEAC), and the schools had to find new premises.

The Thornhill Schools moved to a new building on the site of the present school in Lower Bridge Street. The private school, under its master 'Professor' Holmes, transferred to Cumberland House in Church Street (now Lloyds Bank).

By 1900, the SEAC had become recognised as a School of the University of London – designated the School of Agriculture in the Faculty of Science – under AD Hall (later Sir Daniel Hall, FRS) as Principal. In 1902, he was succeeded by Malcolm JR Dunstan, MA. That year, a BSc in Agriculture was introduced and was followed, in 1906, by a BSc in Horticulture. The increase in student numbers meant that the College premises had to expand and a considerable amount of new building was undertaken: this included a library, laboratories, a gymnasium and a new entrance. Work was completed by the outbreak of WWI in August 1914 but, with many of the students already in the army or navy, the College opened in October with only half the expected number of students, and the new buildings could not be put into use.

MJR Dunstan was able to get state aid to keep the college open and working for the war effort, and he made the gymnasium available for social and fund-raising activities.

The new frontage of the South Eastern Agricultural College after its completion in 1914. Several old cottages on the High Street near the corner with Olantigh Road were demolished to make way for the new buildings and the garden.

Left: Cecil Henry Hooper, his wife and family, c.1912. In front is his daughter Hildegarde. After WW I, she was Mistress of the Girl Guides who met upstairs at Church House in Bridge Street.

'Daddy' Hooper or 'Professor' Hooper, as he was known locally, was Librarian at Wye College from 1907 to 1936. Earlier, he had been a lecturer at Swanley College. He was a keen fossil hunter and naturalist. In May 1924, he was elected Fellow of the Linnaean Society.

CH Hooper was also a surveyor, land agent and valuer; he was very interested in Wye's past history and took an active part in Wye Historical Society. His wife was Canadian, and his daughter Hildegarde became Mrs Sykes, founder Chairman of Tenterden and District Historical Society.

Oxenturn House: front *(above)*, rear *(right)*, c. 1912. This was the home of CH Hooper, Librarian at Wye College. The house became Wye High School in 1974, until this closed and it became a private dwelling. It has recently changed hands.

The Lady Joanna Thornhill Schools

Most of the village children attended the Lady Joanna Thornhill School, but left at age 13 or earlier. Only a few were able to go on to secondary education.

William John Ashby was Headmaster of the Lady Joanna Thornhill Schools from 1900 to 1927, except for four years (November 1915 to February 1919) during WWI when he was serving with the Buffs. During his absence, the school was run by C Blunt. Mrs Ashby was Assistant Mistress from 1910 to 1921. The Ashbys and their four children lived in the schoolhouse – which stood where the school hall is today. They were very active in all aspects of village life and were known for their fine singing voices. From 1903 to 1907, W J Ashby, acted as choir master at Wye Church and he was Secretary of the Temperance Society. He also served as Secretary to the Cottage Gardeners' Society; and played the drums in the Wye Town Band. Outside school hours, he held classes in fretwork and encouraged the boys to take part in sports and to develop an interest in gardening.

The Thornhill School buildings and grounds were also used for local social occasions.

Left: Display of vegetables at the Thornhill School. This display won Wye Cottage Gardeners' Society the challenge cup for the best collection of nine vegetables, for the third time, in November 1909.

Wye gardeners successfully competed against other societies throughout Kent. Everyone - including the SEAC - sent in their best specimens: John Bond made a final selection and organised the display.

Wye also had several private schools to which children came from the surrounding areas.

Right: Staff and boys of one of Wye's private schools in the garden of 6 Church Street, c. 1910. Was this a school run by the Misses McGregor who had previously owned a school in Holly House, Bridge Street? (The Rev. SH Rendall is 5th from the right, and W Lewin 3rd from the right in the back row).

Wye Town Brass Band

Wye Town Band was formed in 1912 by MJR Dunstan, Principal of Wye College. The players were recruited chiefly from Wye and many had no previous experience. The band performed at most village functions, including the annual flower show and fete held on Horton Field, and took part in local and county competitions. During WW I, although depleted in numbers, it performed at various events; including several funerals. On occasion, it took the place of the Church organ.

MJR Dunstan was Band President until 1922, when he left Wye to become Principal of the Royal Agricultural College, Cirencester, and was succeeded by FV Theobald. In 1920, C Greenstreet was succeeded as Bandmaster by W Thorne who, in turn, was followed by his nephew, HJ Picton.

The band reached its peak in the post-war years when it won the Nevill Cup at the Kent Festival of Music for three years in succession (1922-4).

Dunstan was very concerned with village affairs and started a football club for the young men in 1908. There were senior Wednesday and Saturday teams and a junior team. Many band members were also in one or more of the football teams. WJ Ashby, and Canon Lambert, coached the boys.

Wye Cricket Club had been formed much earlier – in 1882. At first, matches were played on the race course at Harville or at Luckley (now Little Chequers). Later, the club was granted permission to use Horton Meadow (the present Cricket Field) which it was able to purchase in the 1960s.

Wye Town Brass Band c. 1913 taken in the Old Vicarage garden. WJ Ashby can be seen with the drums. Behind him is C Greenstreet, the band's conductor. MJR Dunstan, Principal of Wye College, founder and Band President, is on Ashby's right.

Left to right: Unknown, C Burchett, B Burnham, A R Wood.
W Reynolds, W Maxted, Unknown; H J Picton, C Greenstreet, T Butcher, Unknown P Hover, T Brenchley, B Reynolds
J Chittenden, B Penells, G R Hollands, M J R Dunstan, W J Ashby, W Thorne, Unknown, A Lepper, F Boys
A P Masters; J Allard, W Allard, S Reynolds

23

Wye Cricket Club, c. 1914, outside the pavilion on Horton Meadow.

Standing: PC Grey, Unknown, H Godden, W Maxted, J King, AC Pemble, B Reynolds; *Seated:* H Bull, W Lewin (Sec.),
H Mummery; *and in front*, ES Ruck, A Mills?, FS Ruck. (W Lewin was Secretary to the club for over 30 years.)

The senior football team with Arthur Gittings as Captain for the 1913/14 season.

Back row: A Slaughter, J King, Nash, B Reynolds, Unknown, J Rumley. *Seated:* Canon Lambert, Unknown, A Gittings,
W Maxted, H Head. The two men seated in front have not been identified.
Although football was organised through the Church of England Temperance Society from 1902, the Football Club
was started in 1908 by MJR Dunstan; both Arthur Gittings and his brother Walter were members from the beginning
and Arthur presented the club with photographs of the various teams. A new club had to be started after WW I.

The King's Head Hotel

The King's Head Hotel in Church Street was the main centre for social functions in the village, including the annual Football Club dinner.

A fire in 1898, caused by arson, destroyed most of the ancient building behind the Victorian frontage; and Wye Cricket Club lost its equipment which was stored on the premises. The fire had started in the Star Brewery which occupied the site of the present Taylor's Yard. The brewery buildings along Church Street and Clarabut's drapery shop next to the King's Head were also destroyed. Although the hotel and Clarabut's shop were rebuilt, the brewery site remained vacant until purchased by Charles Taylor in 1923 as an addition to his garage on Bridge Street.

(Incidentally, Taylor married the sister of the landlord at the Kings Head.)

Left: Start of a stag hunt outside the Kings Head in Church Street, c. 1912. On the right is the haberdashery and drapers shop owned by Percy Clarabut which became Lewis and Hylands, and is now a branch of the National Westminster Bank.

Until 1925, the hotel was the meeting place for the Court Baron of the local manors subordinate to the Manor of Wye. (These included: Aldon, Brensford, Dodds, Mardoll, Perry, Vicaridge and Westower in Wye; as well as Hinxhill, Boughton Aluph, Kennington and Hothfield). The tenants of these manors had to appear to do 'Suit and Service', to pay dues and to make an Oath of Fealty to the Lord of Wye Manor. CH Hooper was one of those who had to appear, since he leased Oxenturn House, in the manor of Aldon, for a Quit-rent (i.e. a rent which excused the performance of other manorial services, such as working on the farms belonging to the Lord of the Manor).

However, a 'free luncheon' was provided.

The Stag Hunt met in Church Street in front of the King's Head. A stag was released in Oxenturn Road and chased. When caught, it was kept to recover and 'used' on another occasion. The stag 'Charlie' became so tame that it would chase away the sheep when they were being fed at Little Olantigh, and eat their food.

Hunting was an important part of the sporting and social activities of the village and for the students at the SEAC. The East Kent Hunt fox hounds met outside the College for many years.

Even with the increasing use of motor vehicles in the early 1920's, horses were still essential to the rural way of life, both for pleasure and business.

Wye Water Mill

The Domesday survey of 1086 mentions four mills in Wye, and there has probably been a watermill on this site alongside Wye bridge, from at least the 1400's. The present mill house and wheel house, however, date from the 1700's. At the beginning of the century the mill was owned by George Kennett, who sold it in 1906 to Frederick George Harris. Harris already owned the watermill in Brook and the windmill in Wye, (which stood on the site of the present Parish Hall until 1919). In 1919, Thomas Denne purchased the watermill from Harris and it became known as 'Denne's Mill'.

The power to run the machinery came from a large nineteenth century undershot wheel which originally drove four pairs of stones – including a pair for grinding animal feeds. Later, an oil engine was installed to drive the machinery and in 1921 this was replaced by electricity. The machinery was dismantled in 1956 and the buildings were used for storage and became dilapidated. They have recently been acquired for use as a private house and are undergoing extensive restoration.

Harris advertised in Wye Parish Magazine from August 1912 until December 1917.

Right: FG Harris, the miller, outside the watermill at Wye bridge, with his wagon and Shire horses, c.1916. Harris also owned the watermill at Brook and the windmill in Wye; and is believed to have built 'Windmill House' (now Mitford House, 50 Bridge Street) next to his windmill, c. 1880.

Left: The weir and millpond from Wye bridge, c. 1916. The mill race, leading to the wheel house can be seen on the left. The weir was important for oxygenating the river water; and because of the small difference in water levels, the stones were driven by an undershot wheel. Later an oil engine was installed to power the machinery and this was replaced in 1921 by electricity.

Transport

In the early part of the century, the miller, other village tradespeople and the local farming families depended on horses, and horse-drawn vehicles for their mobility and transport. Many tradesmen had their own stabling and storage for carts at the rear of their business premises. Carriers such as Nash, Coulter and Gillingham, ran services to Ashford and Canterbury and transported people and goods to and from Wye Station. They also provided vehicles for outings and important occasions, such as weddings and funerals.

Top left: One of Wye's tradesmen? A horse can just be seen in the stable at the end of the garden. The identity of the man is unknown

Above: The fishmonger shows his wares outside Gittings's house. He and his assistant drove out from Ashford in their trap on a regular delivery round.

Left: Women rode sidesaddle and were very well turned out. (Note the damage to the emulsion bottom right).

Bicycles quickly became regarded by the ordinary people as an essential means of transport; and they gave young people the freedom to explore the countryside. Arthur Gittings used his cycle to transport his camera when he visited places outside the village; and local butchers and grocers had delivery cycles for small orders. Cycling provided work in the village: there were several cycle dealers, such as William Back, in Church Street; Alec Edenden, Bridge Street and Charles Taylor, who had a cycle shop on the Green (on the site of the present Post Office) before opening his garage in Bridge Street in 1913.

Above: A new bicycle with Sturmey Archer gears - note the acetylene headlamp.

Below: Gladys Tippen depicts 'Harvest'. There were even competitions for the best decorated bicycle at local fetes. The basket on her cycle is filled with fruit, and she carries a wheatsheaf and sickle. Above her head can be seen a hoop hung with 'fairylights'. These coloured-glass jars held lighted candles and were used to illuminate the Crown on the Downs above Wye on Guy Fawkes's night and other festive occasions, such as the coronations of Edward VII and George V.

Above: Lily Allard with her bicycle.
Lily worked as a nanny for a milliner's family in Tenterden and probably rode there from Wye on her cycle. She is standing in front of the high wall that ran up Bridge Street from the mill, across what is now Dennes Mill Close.
Lily's father ran the gas works in Lower Bridge Street. His family lived in the 'Gas House', now 'Blackfords'. Because of this, his son William was given the nickname of 'Gassy Allard' at school.

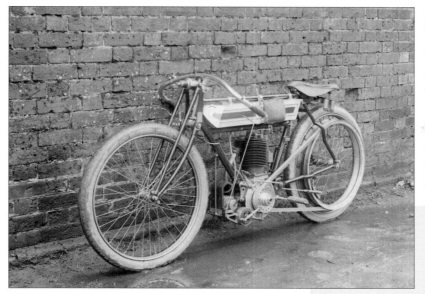

Increasing mechanization inevitably resulted in new problems on the roads, and the police had to spend more time directing traffic which was particularly heavy on race days. But, there were some benefits. Motorcycles with side-cars were introduced by the Post Office in 1914 and must, at least, have improved the postman's lot.

Above: An early motorcycle, possibly a Douglas. (Note the drive belt.) Motorcycles were expensive but fast; they gave the young men, in particular, the means of long-distance travel.

Right: David Beach the Postman with his new motorcycle and sidecar, c. 1914. He and his wife, Eleanor, lived on the Green. Henry Mummery was postmaster and owned the Post Office and stationers' at the corner of the Green and Church Street. H Mummery published and sold many of Gittings's postcards.

Left: Sergeant Harling (c.1916) was one of two village policemen. He was an active member of Wye Cottage Gardeners' Society and continued to win prizes, and to act as a judge for produce at their shows, well into his retirement. His daughters, Ella and Ethel, (later Mrs Hawke and Mrs Greenstreet) were two of a number of local girls who joined the Royal Flying Corps at the aerodrome on Bramble Lane during WWI. Ella joined the RFC at the early age of 16 and worked as a sailmaker, sewing and preparing the fabric with which the planes were covered, and Ethel was a telephonist. (Note the telegraph pole).

In the early part of the century, only the wealthy could afford to own cars. The Principal of Wye College, MJR Dunstan owned a Rolls Royce and the Loudons at Olantigh had several cars and a chauffeur. However, many of the students at the College came from landed or well-to-do professional families, and Wye probably saw more cars than other rural areas. Dealing in vehicles, selling petrol and carrying out repairs brought money into the village and businesses developed to provide these services. Charles Taylor, opened his garage in Bridge Street, between Church House (now Swan House) and the Swan public house, which was until recently the offices of an estate agent.

Above: Harry Southgate, chauffeur at Olantigh.

Left: Line-up of the College Car Club outside Wye Church, c. 1913. MJR Dunstan *(fifth left)* in his Rolls. Car rallies were a popular pastime among young men who enjoyed the thrill of driving fast along the country roads. (The College can be seen in the background.)

In 1908, after several disastrous fires, including the destruction of Olantigh Towers, Wye decided to form its own Fire Brigade. Until then, the village had had to depend on the Ashford Brigade and its horse-drawn engine. By the time it was summoned and had reached Wye, it was usually too late.

A manual fire engine was acquired in 1909 and kept in a shed (where the petrol pumps now stand in front of Taylors Garage). The Fire Brigade was financed entirely by public subscription and local fund-raising activities – including Guy Fawkes's night celebrations. In 1910, a fete was held to raise money to provide uniforms for the firemen; and in September 1912 an additional plot of land on Bridge Street was purchased from WES Erle-Drax for a two-storey building to house a new, and larger, engine. Charles Taylor was able to lease part of this plot for his garage.

Right: Adam John Amos, Captain of the Wye Fire Brigade, showing off his new uniform ? (c. 1910). He stands outside Wye College where he worked as boilerman, and later, as electrician. Adam Amos was very deaf and when the maroon went up to warn of a fire, he was unable to hear it and someone else had to alert him. The horses then had to be fetched from Coulter's field at the end of Cherry Garden Lane, taken to the fire station in Bridge Street, and harnessed up to the fire engine before it could set off to fight the fire.

Some buildings have disappeared since Gittings took his photographs - not only through destruction by fire - and considerable building took place in the centre of Wye during, and after, the 1920s.

The firm of WH Lepper and Sons built houses along Scotton Street and developed the site of the old gas works on the north side of Lower Bridge Street: later, they built the houses on the bank.

Above: The old Work House, which stood on Bridge Street alongside the footpath leading to the Churchfield, is shown on the Plan of Wye Town 1746. At the time this photograph was taken, there was a market garden, opposite, below the alley. The site was later developed by the firm of WH Lepper and Sons.

Right: 'Spiders Castle' Naccolt, c. 1914. The origin of the name is uncertain but it occurs on early maps.

The house, shown here, was owned by Naccolt Brick and Tile Co. which became Ashford and District Brick Co. It stood along the lane running west from Griffin Corner on the road to Wye. Later the house was divided into two, became derelict and was pulled down. The family is possibly Mrs Carpenter and her daughters.

The approach of the First World War

In the years preceding WWI general unrest in Europe prompted the formation of the Territorial Army out of existing auxiliary and volunteer forces in the UK. The Wye section of the Territorial Army was formed in March 1909 and was soon joining other groups at training camps. The Army was also developing the potential of airships and early planes for use in the event of war. Arthur Gittings took a series of photographs of the TA leading church parades through Wye, and he recorded the airship Delta when it flew over Chilham during 1913, attracting 'huge, excited crowds'.

Immediately war was declared on the 4 August 1914, the Wye Scout Master asked for volunteers among the Scouts to act as 'spotters' and to run errands in the neighbourhood. These duties included noting the numberplates of cars on the road between Ashford and Chilham! By late August, Wye Parish Magazine reported that already 122 Wye men were serving in some capacity; twenty-one had already enlisted in the Navy or regular Army and, by December, this number had increased to seventy-five.

Above: The airship Delta at Chilham in July 1913. This was the 4th of 5 non-rigid airships built for the Army before WW I at Barrow-in Furness. Delta was commissioned at Farnborough in 1910 and made her first flight in 1912. During 1913, she took part in numerous manoeuvres, made wireless transmissions, including transmissions to her sistership, Eta, at ranges up to 30miles and, in October, Major EM Maitland made a parachute jump from her at a height of 1800ft over Farnborough. In January 1914 she passed into Admiralty control, and obscurity. During WWI, a later (rigid) airship of the Royal Navy Air Service was stationed at Godmersham and used for surveillance over the Channel.

Territorial church parade at Wye, 1914. The parade is coming from Church Street; past the churchyard on the right and the 'Old Tea Room', (now an Indian restaurant) on the left. There was no house on the Pound. and only a footpath where Churchfield Way is now.

Above: The First Troop Wye Boy Scouts, outside the Lady Joanna Thornhill School in 1914, when G H Garrad, the scoutmaster, left Wye to become Agriculture Administrator for Kent. The scouts acted as messengers and 'spotters' during WW I and were instructed in signalling by J Bilfee, who had been in the Royal Navy.

The following is a quote from the Parish Magazine of November 1914:
'Since the outbreak of the War this Troop has proved itself extremely useful both to Local and Police Authorities. Among their duties may be mentioned the following :— Guarding the telegraph wires, bridges, culverts, etc., between Ashford and Chilham, acting as "patients" to the V.A.D., helping roll bandages at college with Red Cross, collecting "jumble" for the recent Nursing Association sale, and distributing notices for the Refugee Committee.'

Local lads, c. 1916. Conscription came in in 1916 and young men had to enlist at eighteen.

Above: The Ashby family. WJ Ashby was Headmaster of the Lady Joanna Thornhill School. He enlisted in the Buffs in November 1915 and served for 4 years to February1919. His wife was also Mistress at the school and the family lived in the schoolhouse, which was pulled down during WWII, but stood on the site of the present school hall.

Behind Ashby and his wife are their daughters; Blanche, Dorothy and Gladys. Their son, Bill Ashby became a policeman at Margate, and married the sister of cricketer Leslie Ames. *(This negative was badly damaged).*

Above: Harry Southgate, chauffeur at Olantigh, was also called up and became a driver with the army

Above: Wye College members of the Buffs. Wye college had its own special F Company of the 5th Battalion of the Buffs.

Students of Wye College also enlisted. In August 1914, fifty-two members of Wye college joined the Buffs and by the start of the autumn term, 106 of 246 students were in the Army or Navy. The College Principal, MJR Dunstan, realised that many local people depended on the income they received from providing lodgings for the students, and he made arrangements for servicemen to be billeted with families in the village or nearby.

During the course of WWI, Wye was host to nearly four hundred military personnel. The first to arrive were men of A Squadron 9th Cavalry Reserves, a contingent of the 3rd Kings Own Hussars. They were billeted in Wye from January to April 1915, and their horses were stabled at neighbouring farms. The Hussars were followed by men of the Lancashire Field Ambulance Corps and the Army Medical Corps; and a hospital was established in the College museum. During 1916 the Royal Flying Corps moved into the aerodrome that had been built along the northern side of Bramble Lane, west of the railway line. Other troops were billeted in the village later in the war.

Cavalry men with their hosts. (The identity of the couple is unknown).

Cavalry at Harville. The stables at the racecourse were used to house the horses.
The men have just finished 'mucking out'. (Note the grooming brushes).

Above A Trooper in the 3rd Kings Own Hussars, under 'Fighting Orders'. Note the 9-pouch bandolier with rifle ammunition, cavalry sword and rifle in the 'bucket' on the far side. The horse is branded with the 'arrow' marking Government Property.

Above: A Trooper under 'Marching Orders'. The photograph was taken outside Taylor's Garage, Bridge Street. Note, the water bottle, haversack and spare kit, and, behind the sword, the wooden pegs to which the horse could be tethered.

Above: Cavalry man, with village lad dressed up ? The two are wearing an early version of service dress with reinforced patches on the shoulders. This, and the obsolete, pre-WWI rifle (a long Lee-Enfield) suggest that this was a second-line unit. (Note the steel helmets and the small box respirators).

Although the money the servicemen had to spend was vital to the village economy, they helped the community in many other ways. Some sang in the church choir or rang the bells; and even acted as organist. They put on entertainments to raise funds for village activities and trained the boys in gymnastics. Many friendships were formed with Wye people; and some of the young men met and married local girls.

Above: The team of the A Squadron 9th Cavalry Reserve Football Club with senior NCOs. The men helped to organise gymnastic training and sports for the village boys.

The Volunteer Training Corps and Territorial Army in Wye

Those Wye men who were not eligible to go on active service were nevertheless engaged in the war effort. They worked on the land (Charles Taylor drove a tractor) or spent their non-working hours in auxiliary organisations at home. Many joined the Volunteer Training Corps or the TA: they included WES Erle-Drax, MJR Dunstan and CH Hooper. There seemed to be no age restriction; and some of the young lads also enlisted.

At the outbreak of war ten members of the parish were serving in the TA, twenty in the National Reserve and seventy-one were Special Constables. The Wye Platoon of the Volunteer Training Corps was formed in November 1916 and came under new War Office regulations in February 1917, which specified the type of training recruits should receive. Regular camps, drills, route marches and training sessions with other local groups started. But attendance was a problem. To quote from the Parish Magazine, 'the demands of allotments and gardens have entailed late drills in the evenings' but, regulation rifle practice revealed that the platoon contained 'several promising shots'. By December every volunteer was supplied with a service rifle and equipment, but uniforms came 'along by degrees'. Duties included guarding special installations against sabotage, and making preparations to repel invaders. (Very similar to those of the Home Guard in the Second World War).

In May 1918, the Wye Battalion (the 8th Battalion of the Kent Volunteer Regiment) became the 4th Volunteer Battalion of the Buffs (East Kent Regiment) and in September numbered nearly forty men. After the Armistice in November 1918, it was noted that seventeen former members of the Volunteer Force had enlisted in the Army and one had joined the Navy, during the course of the war; one had been killed and three wounded.

Men of the Volunteer Training Corps (Territorials) with WES Erle-Drax outside 'Glenthorne'– now James Wyllie House, Upper Bridge Street, Wye (22 November 1916).
WES Erle-Drax *(centre, middle row)*; next to him on the right, Alfred Lepper. C H Hooper, the College Librarian *(Back row no 3)*, served with the Kent Cyclist Battalion; John Bond, head gardener at Olantigh, is on his right.

The Wye War Hospital Supply Depot

The WWHSD was started by Florence Barnard of Withersdane Hall in November 1914. It became established in the College and is commemorated by the following inscription over the centre doorway in the middle quad:

**' DURING THE GREAT WAR *1914-1918*.
THE WYE WAR HOSPITAL SUPPLY DEPOT
WORKED IN THIS BUILDING FOR THE WOUNDED OF THE ALLIED ARMIES.'**

By the end of 1917, over 65,000 items had been made and dispatched to hospitals at home and at the Front. These included: bandages, swabs, gauze compresses and hospital clothing.

The Depot was only the second of its kind in the UK. Hester Dunstan, the Principal's daughter, had attended a training course in Ipswich and provided the technical expertise. The women of Wye gave their time and labour. This was a considerable commitment for them, alongside their other duties of caring for their families and the servicemen billeted with them; and the necessity of keeping family businesses running in the absence of their menfolk. The Depot also relied entirely for its funding on money-raising events and donations from the local community.

Below: WWHSD voluntary workers, after 30 women and one man were presented with official badges (V.W. surmounted by a crown) from the Director General of Voluntary Organisations, on 10 May 1916; with 'our local photographer' in attendance.
Centre back, standing: Mrs Florence Barnard, chief organiser, with Andrew Bigoe Barnard. *Seated:* Mrs Dunstan.
Right Back, standing: Jennie Austin with M. and Mdme Arnoux, two of the Belgian refugees who were housed in the village.

Left: Ambulance of the Voluntary Aid Detachment, Army Service Corps, c.1916. The driver wears the uniform of the West Lancashire Field Ambulance Corps. During this period, the College museum became a hospital for the Royal Army Medical Corps whose members were also billeted with families in the village.

During WWI, a searchlight was located on the Downs above Fanscombe and the servicemen who manned this were billeted with the Hann family at Little Olantigh. Having these young men living with them affected the family in several ways: one of the soldiers developed rheumatic fever and had to be taken to hospital; but not before Annie Hann had contracted the disease. With no antibiotics to counter the infection, it damaged her heart and eventually led to her death. More happily, one of the older sisters, Florence, met and married Alfred Phillips.

Above: The family of Elizabeth and Edwin Hann with the Searchlight Team outside Little Olantigh Farmhouse, c. 1915. *Back row: 1,2 and 4,* 2nd Hussars; *3,* 6th Dragoon Guards; and *5,* 7th Hussars. *Middle:* Gladys, Bill (Will), Annie, *Front:* Hilda, Elizabeth Hann with baby Irene, Edwin Hann and George. (The soldier *back left* developed rheumatic fever.)

Wedding group of Florence May Hann and Alfred Henry Phillips (Private, 3rd Hussars),
22 December 1917, outside the farmhouse at Little Olantigh.

Back row: Edwin Hann, Annie, a cousin - name unknown, Edward, Gladys, Will,
Front: Hilda, Elizabeth Hann with Irene, Alfred Phillips with George Hann, Florence, Dorothy and Jack.

The Royal Flying Corps

Men of the Royal Flying Corps, parading across Wye bridge from the station past Gittings's house and shop on their way to church during 1916. Gittings's house was lower than the road and could be flooded when water ran down Bridge Street. Photographs can be seen in the end window of his shop. Note the station buildings and houses on Harville Road. On the left is the large granary building belonging to the mill which was partly demolished when Dennes Mill Close was developed, and has recently been rebuilt as offices.

'The Hut', on Harville Road opposite Wye station, was run under the auspices of the Church of England Temperance Society as a club for the servicemen stationed in Wye. It originally came from Shornecliffe Camp, and after WW1 was used as a meeting place for various village organisations until the Public Hall was opened in October 1921, when the Hut was sold to help meet expenses. The band of lady volunteers were organised by Miss Amos; tea and coffee were served but no alcohol and the club closed at 10pm !

Preparations for the '*al fresco* concert' which followed a ' wonderful display of flying ' at the Aerodrome, 10 August 1916. The stage was erected in the Officers' Mess. The Parish Magazine reports, 'the RFC band appeared on a pretty stage with scenery representing a view of the church looking up Church Street'. The backcloth had been painted by Mrs Dunstan for a previous entertainment. Proceeds from the concert were given to the village social fund. After WW1 this hangar was bought for £350 and re-erected next to Swan House, Bridge Street, to serve as a Public Hall. It was later sold to C Taylor as an extension for his garage.

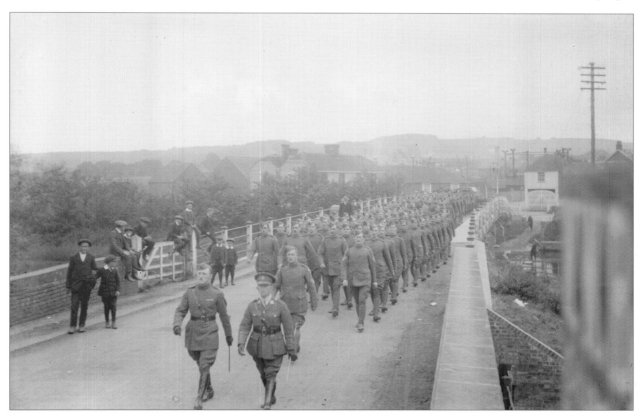

The RFC returning from church parade. The Victoria Inn, its outbuildings and Gittings's house can be seen on the left of the bridge and the old granary building on the right. Behind this is the gas holder and chimney of Wye gas works in Lower Bridge Street. Wye church, the Crown and chalk pit are just visible in the distance.

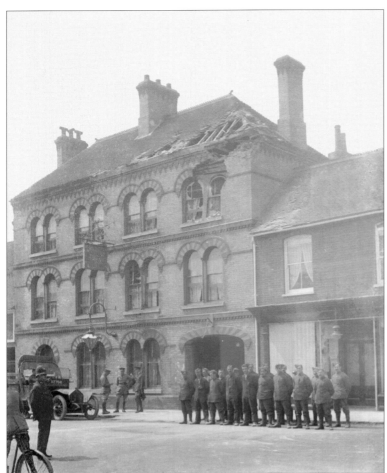

Above: Training mishap: plane in a tree on the Green.

Left: Line up for the enquiry following an accident when a plane hit the King's Head, July 1916. The young pilot was dropping confetti at the marriage of his colleague, Captain Arthur Downton and Miss Joan Dunstan, daughter of the Principal of Wye College. He flew too low over the church and crashed into the King' Head Hotel, but was not seriously injured. Not all the pilots were so lucky !

Pilots of the RFC passing the forecourt of the Victoria Inn, 25 October 1916, on their way to the funeral of Cecil E Tombs of the RFC who died in an accident, aged 20. He was buried with full military honours in Wye churchyard – where his headstone can still be seen. Wye mill is on the left and the Hut can just be seen on the other side of the bridge. The pilots were recruited from various regiments. (Note the cycles and carts and the child riding on the rear axle of the carriage).

The young pilots were daring: they had accidents, sometimes fatal, and those who died were buried in Wye or neighbouring villages. The other WWI victims in Wye churchyard are those who had been brought home fatally wounded, or ill, as a result of service overseas. In addition to their grief when loved ones at the Front were killed or injured, for the first time people had to cope with the risk of injury to themselves or their children, and the possibility of damage to their homes as a result of enemy bombing. Blackout had been imposed in 1915; and in June 1917, C Blunt was concerned for the safety of children at the Thornhill Schools, in the event of air raids.

Above: The grave of Lance Corporal Percy Amos, 2/4 the Buffs, in Wye Churchyard. He was the son of Stephen and Sarah Amos of White Hill. and died of wounds, 25 November 1916. At that time, there was an uninterrupted view across the Churchfield.

Above: The grave of Private G JC van Rooyen of the 5th Buffs, with the College buildings behind. He was the first student of the Agricultural College to be buried in Wye Churchyard, on 1 November 1915.

Right: WWI bomb damage. The plaque between the windows of the nearest houses identifies them as 'Jubilee Cottages'.
(This was probably the row of cottages of that name which stood at the far end of Black Griffin Lane, Canterbury).

Because he was excused war service, Arthur Gittings was able to be present at most of the wartime weddings. Despite, or perhaps, because of knowing the risks, some couples decided to marry during WWI before the men returned to the Front. The bridegroom was almost always in uniform.

Such a couple were Canon Lambert's daughter, Rachel, and Lieutenant Christopher Bushell who married at Wye church on 24 August 1915.

Lieutenant Bushell served with the Queen's Royal West Surrey Regiment. He commanded the 7th Battalion in France during 1917 and was 'mentioned twice in Sir D Haig's despatches'. In May 1918 he was presented with both the DSO and the VC 'for most conspicuous bravery and devotion to duty when in command of his battalion'. He was promoted to Lieutenant-Colonel. Tragically he fell leading his men on 8 August 1918 – not long before the Armistice.

Wedding group following the marriage of Lieutenant Christopher Bushell and Miss Rachel Lambert (the Vicar's daughter) 24th August 1915, outside the Principal's house, Wye College. This was a gathering of all of Wye 'society'.

Key above: 1, WES Erle-Drax; 2, Miss Hilda Lambert; 3, B Barnard; 4, unknown; 5, Miss Biddlecombe; 6, Mrs Lambert's sister; 7, Mrs Loudon; 8, Miss Dorothy Erle-Drax; 9, Mrs Barnard; 10, Miss Margaret Erle-Drax; 11, unknown; 12, unknown; 13, Mrs Dunstan, with parrot; 14, MJR Dunstan; 15, Canon Lambert; 16, Mrs Lambert; 17, Rachel Lambert; 18, Lieut C Bushell; 19, Mrs Bushell; 20, Mrs Bushell's sister; 21, Norman Barnard; 22, Joanna Barnard; 23, Rosamond Barnard; 24, Roger Lambert; 25, Stephen Lambert; 26, Billy Loudon; 27, Denis Lambert; 28, Pamela Haines; 29, ? Haines.

The bride is Myrtie Southfield whose father, Frederick, was tenant farmer at Hunt Street. The groom is Hector Naylor of Sutton Farm, near Pett Street, (now demolished). The couple married during 1915 at Crundale Church.

Wedding of one of Wye's sailors. The identity of this couple is not known; but the photograph is a reminder that a number of Wye men served in the RN during WW I. The groom was based at Chatham (hence, 'HMS *Pembroke*' on his hat band).

Many couples waited until after the Armistice to get married.

Wedding of Frederick William Barnard, Corporal, RAF to Bertha May Maskell on February 22nd 1919. The couple are pictured with the bride's parents and brother, Private W Maskell, behind 65 Bridge Street, where her family lived.

Wedding of one of Wye's WAAFs. Unusually, it is the bride who is in uniform. The photograph was probably taken late 1918 or 1919 after the RAF and WAAF were formed from the RFC. It is clearly post WWI, since both of the young men wear silver war medals. (The identities are not known).

After the War

After the Armistice on 11 November 1918, life in Wye continued much as it had during the war. It was a time of great stringency; but, gradually, men were starting to return to their families and, in January 1919, the Vicar, Canon Lambert, wrote 'The wonderful year of Victory has passed and now we have entered on what, we trust, will be a still more wonderful time of peace and reconconstruction.'

Peace celebrations were held on 6 July 1919 on the racecourse, (Arthur Gittings came third in a 150 yd race for men aged between 30 and 40). In the evening the Crown, which had been specially cleaned by members of the Girls' Club, was illuminated and there was a dance at the Hut. The WI gave a party for men from the aerodrome and the artillery camp with 200 guests 'and a very happy merry evening was spent'.

The community decided to build a memorial in the churchyard to Wye's war dead; and to revive the proposal, held in abeyance during WWI, for a Public Hall. These projects required an estimated £1,500, to be raised by public donation. Some £1,368 was collected, and Wye War Memorial to 29 men from the village, was dedicated on 17 March 1921. A further 127 students and staff from the SEAC who lost their lives in WWI, are commemorated on a memorial at the College (Mrs Dunstan carved the crest on the panel).

The hangar used as the Officers' Mess at the aerodrome, was moved to the site adjoining Taylor's Garage, refurbished, and opened as Wye Public Hall, in October 1921. It remained in use until the present Village Hall was built in the late 1930s, when it was sold to Taylor's Garage.

Money was also urgently needed to help those wounded or blinded in the war, and despite the general poverty, fund-raising events took place and money was forthcoming. People even donated vegetables for the crews of minesweepers based at Dover; and for a canteen set up in Church House, Bridge Street, to provide lunches for village schoolchildren.

Opposite right: Len and Betty Foster (with sunflowers). Their father, Sergeant Foster of the Leicestershire Regiment was drafted to India and died in France in June 1915, of wounds received in Mesopotamia. His family had accompanied him to India and after his death returned to Wye. His wife Lizzie (born Lizzie Greenstreet) became District Nurse after Nurse Martin's retirement in 1916. When adult, Len Foster joined the Fleet Air Arm, but contracted TB and died in 1936 at the age of twenty-six.

Wye Church from the church gate showing the War Memorial dedicated 17 March 1921. Twenty-nine men from Wye lost their lives during WWI. This photograph was used for the cover of the Parish Magazine from June 1923. Churchfield Way had not yet been built.

In the years after the war, the production of food continued to be a priority. The College ran courses on efficient land management; and the regular displays and competitions put on by the Wye Cottage Gardeners' Society served to encourage people to make good use of their gardens and allotments and to produce more.

The W I, which had been founded on 18 June 1917, with Mrs Dunstan as President, played a leading role in educating local women in the preparation of food, and a jam factory was started. Women were exhorted to take an active part in growing vegetables; and when the Cottage Gardeners' Society made WI women honorary members in 1918, Mrs Dunstan was the first woman to join. (Arthur Gittings was elected on the same occasion and went on to compete successfully in some of the competitions).

Above: Tommy Dodd, the 'Rhubarb King' (c. 1918) in the yard behind his house at 125 Bridge Street, Wye. He was an active member of the Wye Cottage Gardeners' Society, won many prizes for his produce and was frequently called on to judge at the monthly meetings. In 1918, he won the prize for the 'best' rhubarb for the 25th consecutive year, and continued to win for at least another seven years. In 1921, his sticks were '46ins long and and 5ins round'.

Although he had originally trained in horticulture, Tommy Dodd became a pork butcher during the 1890s, and people brought their pigs for him to slaughter in the yard behind his house. In 1893 he was chopping wood when a splinter flew up, lodged in his eye and blinded him; and he was given a glass eye.

Left: Exhibits at the Kent Honey Show. The Kent Honey Show was held annually at Wye until 1922, usually in a marquee on Horton Meadow during the annual flower show and village sports; but, sometimes at the SEAC. On occasion, there were 300 or more exhibitors.

Right: Prize rabbits ? Rabbits, both wild and domestic formed an important item in the diet; they also provided skins for clothing. The leases of some of the older properties in Wye stipulated how many rabbits were allowed to be kept. In 1918, the WI advertised the names of local farmers who would supply rabbits: 'Young rabbits at a shilling each for rearing can be obtained from Mr Kempe, Red House, Wye and pure bred ones at 2 shillings each from Mr. Howse, Coldharbour Farm'.

48

As more men came back from active service, life in Wye started to return to normal. One of those who returned was William Lepper, who had enlisted in the RFC, in 1917 aged 45, and was based at Canterbury. He had married Elizabeth Wood, a widow who already had a son, Albert. William and Elizabeth had four sons, Frank Sid, Brian and Denis, and a daughter, Nora. The family lived at 25 the Green and all the children attended the Lady Joanna Thornhill School. Frank and Sid were very keen on cycling and would cycle as far as Southampton to visit relatives. Frank said, 'When we got fed up with biking we got motor cycles and roamed all over the place with them to Scotland and Wales on nice clear roads and although we didn't have much money we seemed to enjoy ourselves'.

Before WWI, William and his brother Alfred had worked for their father [also William] who owned the store and general builders at the beginning of Olantigh Road. After the war, William and Alfred operated a successful building firm and were joined in the business by William's son Frank. The firm of WH Lepper and Sons built many new houses in Wye during the 1920s, notably, along Scotton Street and Lower Bridge Street. They also worked on Olantigh House, Withersdane Hall and many other houses in the area and were responsible for the renovation of 'Yew Trees' in Scotton Street. In 1937 the firm was sold to the Earls, and Frank Lepper, then employed by Headley's, continued to work in Wye until he retired in 1968.

When they were adults, Sid, Brian and Denis worked for Charles Taylor at his garage in Bridge Street, and the business passed into their hands when Taylor died in 1935. Nora Lepper worked at Wye College.

Elizabeth's son, Albert Wood, played the trombone with the Wye Town Band. He was very tall and can be seen in the back row in the photograph of the band taken in 1913 (see page 23). Albert Wood served with the Buffs in WWI, and survived, only to die of pneumonia a few years later. His half-brothers, Brian and Sid Lepper, also joined the band after the war.

The next generation was beginning to be active in village affairs.

Above: William Lepper in RFC uniform, c. 1917. He enlisted when he was 45, and was based at Canterbury.

Above: William and Elizabeth Lepper and family. c. 1919. The family lived at 25, the Green, and the boys were to play an important part in Wye's commercial life. *Back, left to right:* Brian, Frank, Sid, *Front:* Elizabeth with Denis, Nora and William.